BWV 1043, 'Vivace'

Johann Sebastian Bach.

BWV 1043
1st Movement/Vivace
J.S.BACH DOUBLE VIOLIN CONCERTO
in D minor for 4 Guitars
by- Jim Ross

Also available

- 1 FINGER EXERCISES FOR THE FRETTING HAND
- 2 FINGER EXERCISES FOR THE FRETTING HAND
- 3 FINGER EXERCISES FOR THE FRETTING HAND
- 4 FINGER EXERCISES FOR THE FRETTING HAND
- THE 1-2-3-4 FINGER GUITAR SYSTEM COMPLETE

with many more titles available

J.S.Bach Double Violin Concerto in D minor

BWV 1043- 'Vivace'

For information regarding this Book contact: info@jimrossprojects.com

ISBN 978-1-105-98482-2

Please Visit : **www.JIMROSSPROJECTS.com**
for more information, links, music, videos, books, & other material from the author.

This book is dedicated to the genius of

J.S.Bach

1685 - 1750

J.S. Bach's Double Concerto for 2 Solo Violins in D minor transcribed for 4 guitars by -Jim Ross

"Music is an agreeable harmony for the honor of God and the permissible delights of the soul"

-J.S.Bach

PREFACE

This guitar transcription also appears as a conclussion to the 4-part guitar technique Series: "The 1-2-3-4 GUITAR SYSTEM" -by Jim Ross; a system designed to isolate the fretting hand finger groupings to maximize technical efficiency. But this edition also includes an analysis and explanation of my arrangement of the Concerto that was not included in the 4-part Series.

This will give a unique insight to how the guitar and bass guitar parts were arranged, as well as demonstrating how you can adapt my transcription to better suit your preferred '*flow*' across the fretboard. Of course there is usually more than one way to achieve the same results, and in this dedicated book I will explore a few variations of the given themes to demonstrate how you can do just that. Good luck, and have fun!

-Jim Ross

J.S. Bach's Double Concerto for Solo Violin in D minor

his book is a study on J.S. Bach's Double Concerto in Dm for two solo violins that has been transcribed for four guitars. The complete Concerto is made up of 3 sections: Vivace, Allegro, and Largo. The Vivace section is the only one covered in this book, the others are available as well. The goal in this study is to:

1) Analyze specific sections of this piece, using the main re-occuring themes as examples.

2) Learn how to work through any 'trouble-spots', and to work out all of the difficult fingerings.

3) Experiment with alternate positionings, string sequences, & fretting configurations.

THE CONCERTO GUITAR ARRANGEMENT

This is the 1st movement of three in the key of D minor/ F Major. It is the Vivace; meaning it is to be played in a lively, brisk, vivacious manner. There are 88 measures all together and depending on the tempo used, it is about 3 1/2 - 4 1/2 minutes long. Being that it is 'Vivace' you should aim to push the tempo as much as you can; but of course don't try to play it any faster than you can play it cleanly and properly. It is performed in a canon type style, where melodies are echoed and harmonized as they weave in and out of each other.

My guitar transcription was actually derived from notation of two violins & a piano. I interpret this particular piece as something that would be played nicely by a string quartet. So I've arranged it in that type of format.

The two solo violin parts appear here as guitar one and guitar two. I separated the left and right hands of the piano to be played as: doublebass (left hand) and cello (right hand). Of course many possible interpretations can be applied in the way of instrumentation. I've chosen, in this books arrangement, to apply a baritone guitar (which is a guitar tuned from low B^6-E-A-D-F#-B^1 -to the doublebass part, and a standard bass guitar to the cello part. The instrumentation I chose can be changed according to your preference of course.

I chose the baritone guitar mostly because that is how I prefer to tune my main guitar. But also because a lot of low notes drop below the E note; the lowest note on a standard tuned guitar. And of course they do, this is written in D minor so you'd expect a lot of low D notes to occur right? I'd encourage you to create your own arrangements with alternate tunings and fingerings as well.

The cello part could have easily been arranged for baritone guitar instead of bass guitar and vice versa. And honestly since the doublebass is a lower tuned instrument it would make sense to have done it that way. I would have preferred to use a 6 string bass tuned an octave lower than a baritone guitar to perform the doublebass part, but I don't have a 6 string bass, so I applied this transcription to what guitars I have in my studio to work with. But again, I encourage you to re-arrange this Concerto in a way that works best for you. My fingerings are only suggestions of how you could play it. It's not law, of course!

REOCCURING THEMES

First we will examine a few of the themes that appear throughout this piece, and then we will compare the variations as they reoccur. The focus will mainly be on the 2 solo violin parts as they are the staple of the entire piece. But we'll take a few looks at the doublebass & cello parts as well (in the *Alternate Fingering* section) to show the way some of these chords and chord progression move around the fretboard. I will break this Concerto up into 3 main themes:

- **Theme #1 - introduction**
- **Theme #2 - solo section A and B**
- **Theme #3 - sweep section**

****

Theme #1

The 1st measure of Theme #1 occurs 6 times total throughout the Vivace section. It repeats in both of the violin #1 and violin #2 parts, but in different modes and variations. It appears 1st in the opening measure with violin #2 as shown below:.

A) is played in measure 1-2 by violin #2
B) is played in measure 5-6 & 46-47 by violin #1
C) is played in measure 14-15 by violin #2
D) is played in measure 18-19 by violin #1
E) is played in measure 85-86 by violin #1

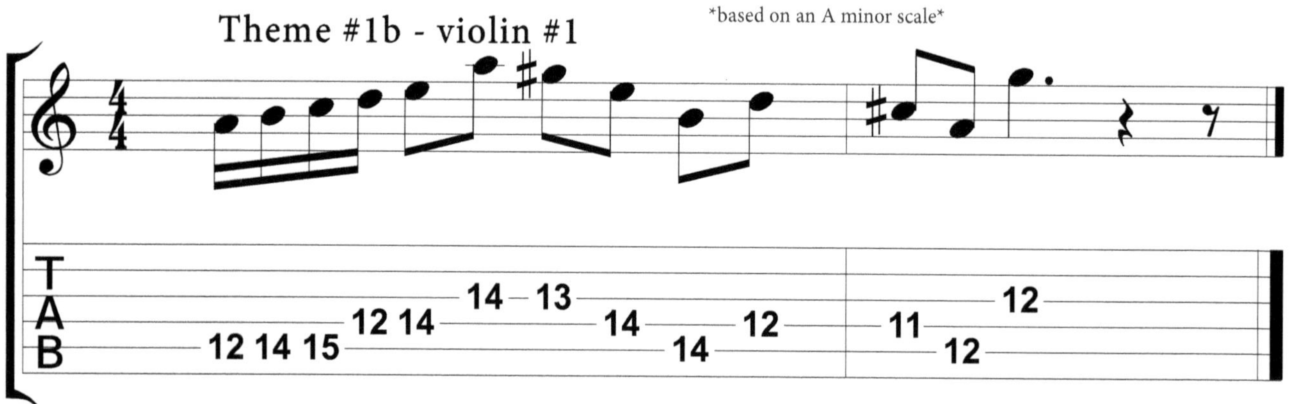

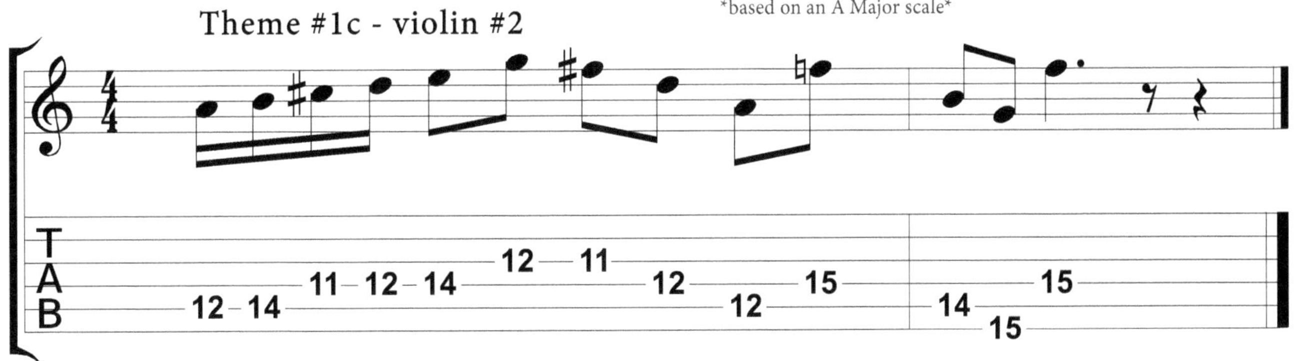

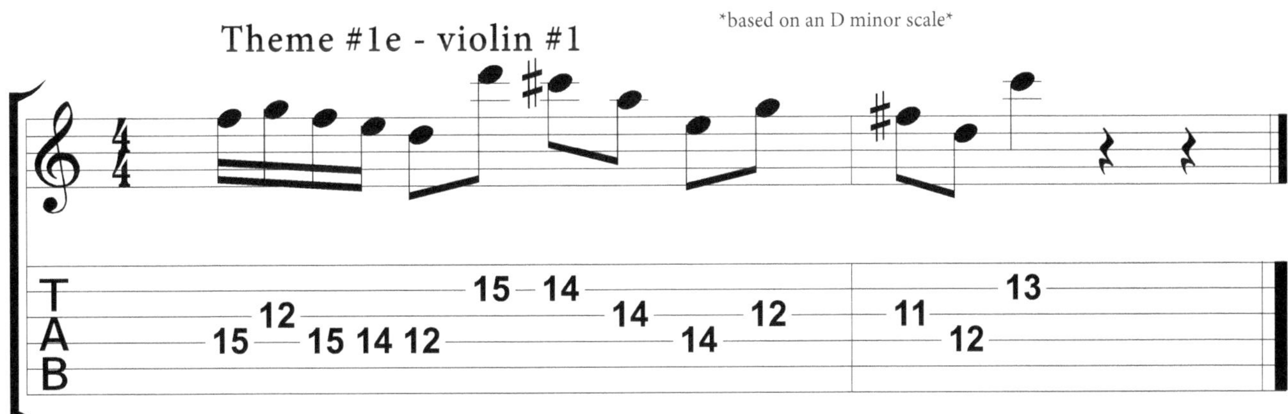

Those are the only times that theme appears. Notice that violin #2 plays first, then violin #1 imitates the theme four bars after in canon, and this happens again in measures 14 through18 in a similar way.

Violin #1 plays this theme by itself without the "canon imitation" from violin #2; once in measure 46, and then plays it again without the canon in measure 85.

Theme #2

Theme #2 is the start of each solo section. The Solo section is started by violin #1 in measure 22 and then imitated in canon by violin #2 four bars later. This format is repeated 3 times, placed towards the begining, middle, and the end of the piece. throughout the course of this Concerto. I'll break the solo sections up into: Solo Section A & Solo Section B for each of the 3 parts. The 1st & 3rd are identical, the 2nd one is different.

Solo section A- is made up of a set of 3 descending 10ths followed by a descending scale.
The doublebass & cello plays the chord accents: Dm-A-Dm / Gm-D-Gm
notice the use of the D Major chord in the key of D minor
Theme #2a, Solo section A appears 4 times with both violin #1 and #2 playing it twice each.
They are played in:

measure 22-23 by violin #1
measure 26-27 by violin #2
measure 77-78 by violin #1
measure 81-82 by violin #2

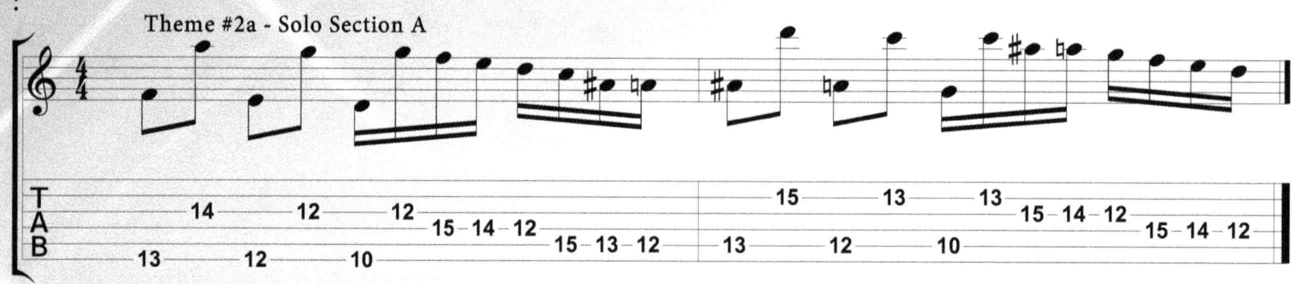

Solo section B- is a nice melody line that follows a series of changing chords every quarter note for 2 bars.
Theme #2a Solo Section B are the 2nd half of each of the Solo Section A measures:

measure 24-25 by violin #1
measure 28-29 by violin #2
measure 79-80 by violin #1
measure 83-84 by violin #2

All 4 times are played exactly the same way (with violin #1 imitated by violin #2 directly after); as shown below:

Theme #2b, Solo Sections A & B are played once by each violin in the middle of the piece.
They are very similar to the Theme #2a Solo Sections, but are played down a 4th this time.

Solo section A- is also made up of a set of 3 descending 10ths followed by a descending scale.
The doublebass & cello plays the chord accents: Am-E-Am / Dm-A-Dm
notice the use of the A Major chord in the key of D minor
Theme #2a, Solo section A appears 4 times with both violin #1 and #2 playing it twice each.
They are played in:

measure 38-39 by violin #2

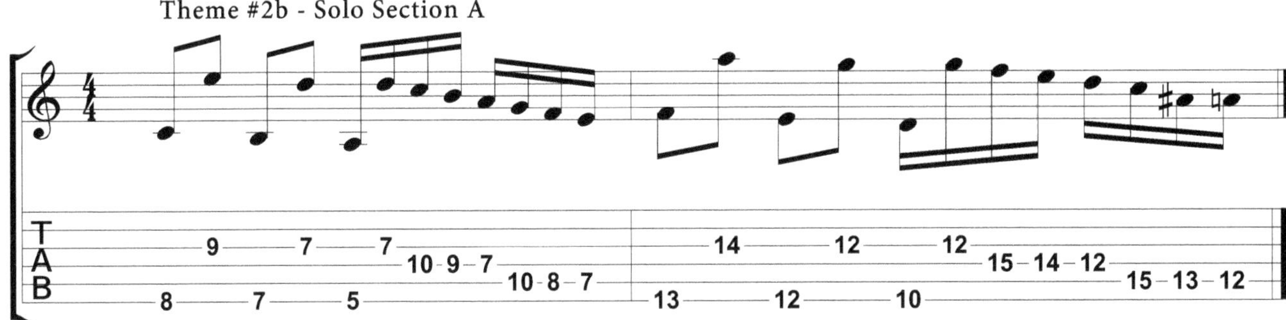

measure 42-43 by violin #1

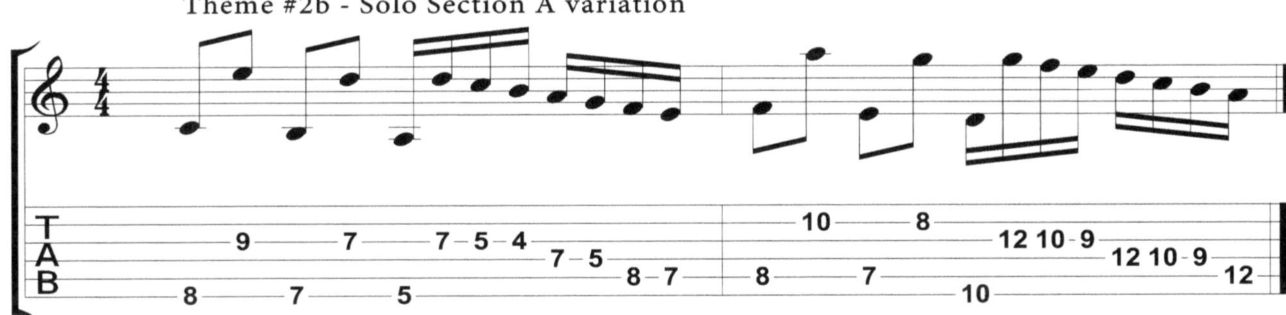

Both examples above are made of the same exact notes. But in order to shift up to the 12th position for Theme #2b, Solo Section B, I tried to work out a way to get up in that position easier. I could have moved the B section to the down to the 7th position, but I wanted to use the same exact position & fingering as it occurs throughout the piece. So that is why I did it like this instead.
The 1st example requires a large position shift going into the 2nd measure, but that sets you up for the familiar fingerings in the following measures. The 2nd example has less of a shift, but takes 2 measures to get to the familiar fingering of Section B. Either way will work & is fine, but we'll explore some alternate possibilities at the end of this book as well.

Solo section B- is a nice melody line that follows a series of changing chords every quarter note for 2 bars.
Theme #2a Solo Section B are the 2nd half of each of the Solo Section A measures:

measure 40-41 by violin #2
measure 44-45 by violin #1

Theme #2b - Solo Section B is the same fingering as Theme #2b -Solo Section B, but it's played a 4th lower.

Theme #3

Theme #3 is made up of two seperate sweep style melodies. The 1st set has two variations: Sweep Run 1 & 2. The 2nd set has 4 variations: Sweep Runs 3, 4, 5 , & 6. This is how I've notated them for this transcription, but I want to encourage you to explore your own variations & fingerings.

SWEEP RUNS 1 & 2

<u>Theme #3, Sweep Run 1</u>- is bascially 4 chords: potentially: Dm - Am - F° - B°
This one is played in measure 36-47 by violin #1, *see below*:

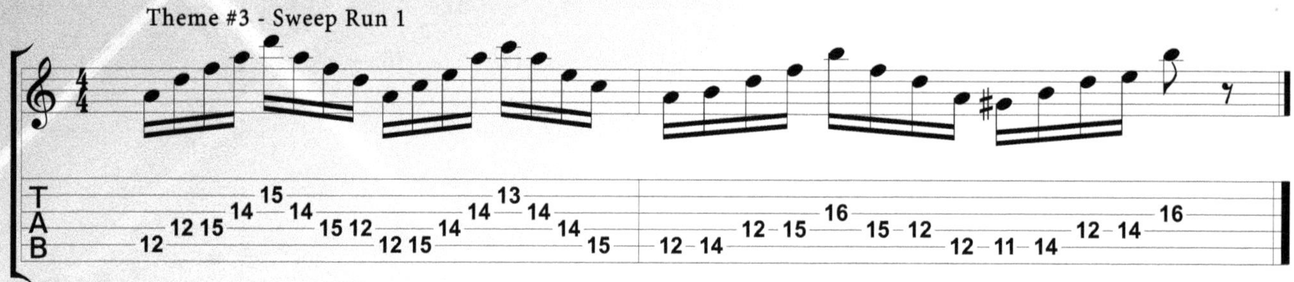

<u>Theme #3, Sweep Run 2</u>- is 4 chords (a 5th lower than Run 1) potentially: Am - Dm - C° - F#°
This one is played in measure 75-76 by violin #2, *see below*:

The next set of 4 Sweep Runs are similar, but the flow is broken up a little differently. You'll see that 3 & 4 are the same basic pattern but are a 4th apart. And likewise, 5 & 6 are the same pattern played a 4th apart from each other. Again, at the end of this book I'll show some other possible ways you could play these. But these will at least get you through each of the sections.

SWEEP RUNS 3, 4, 5, & 6

Theme #3, Sweep Run 3- is played in measure 50-51 by violin #2, *see below*:

Theme #3, Sweep Run 4- is played inmeasure 52-53 by violin #1, *see below*:

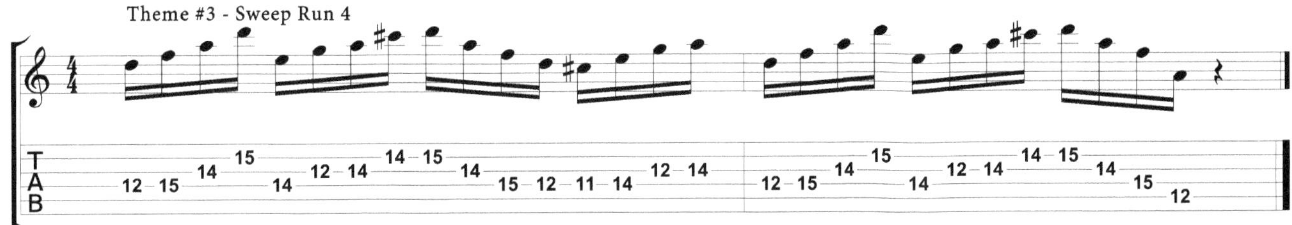

Theme #3, Sweep Run 5- is played in measure 59-60 by violin #1, *see below*:

Theme #3, Sweep Run 6- is played in measure 61-62 by violin #2, *see below*:

Seffner's Statue of J.S. Bach

"I was obliged to be industrious. Whoever is equally industrious will succeed equally well."

-J.S.Bach

J.S. Bach's Double Concerto for Solo Violin in D minor

BWV 1043- 'Vivace'

transcribed for 4 guitars

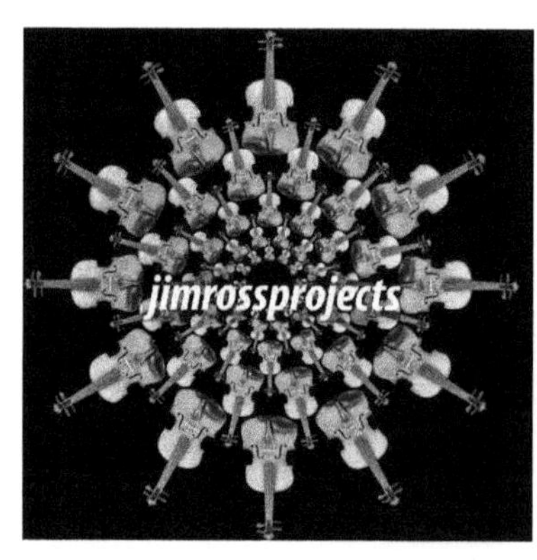

PLAYING THE CONCERTO

So now that you've familiarized yourself with the intricacies of a few of the main themes, you should have a good idea of what you will be playing in the following pages. I've outlined only three various themes, but there are plenty more all through this entire Concerto. Do your best to see the relationship of similar lines & melodies as they occur throughout the following pages.

Let's go ahead and jump right into this! Each part is notated separately 1st, then the complete score will follow those. Then after the score, there will be a section dedicated to the possible variations of fingerings for some of the material. I'd recommend spending some quality time with both the individual parts & the score. There's a lot to be gained from the brilliant works of Bach.

Good luck, and do your best to bring this music to life!

****

violin #1 - standard guitar #1
violin #2 - standard guitar #2
doublebass - baritone guitar (BEADF#B) *or bass*
cello - standard guitar or bass

VIOLIN #1 for standard Guitar

TAB

63
f
65
68
70
72
74
76
78

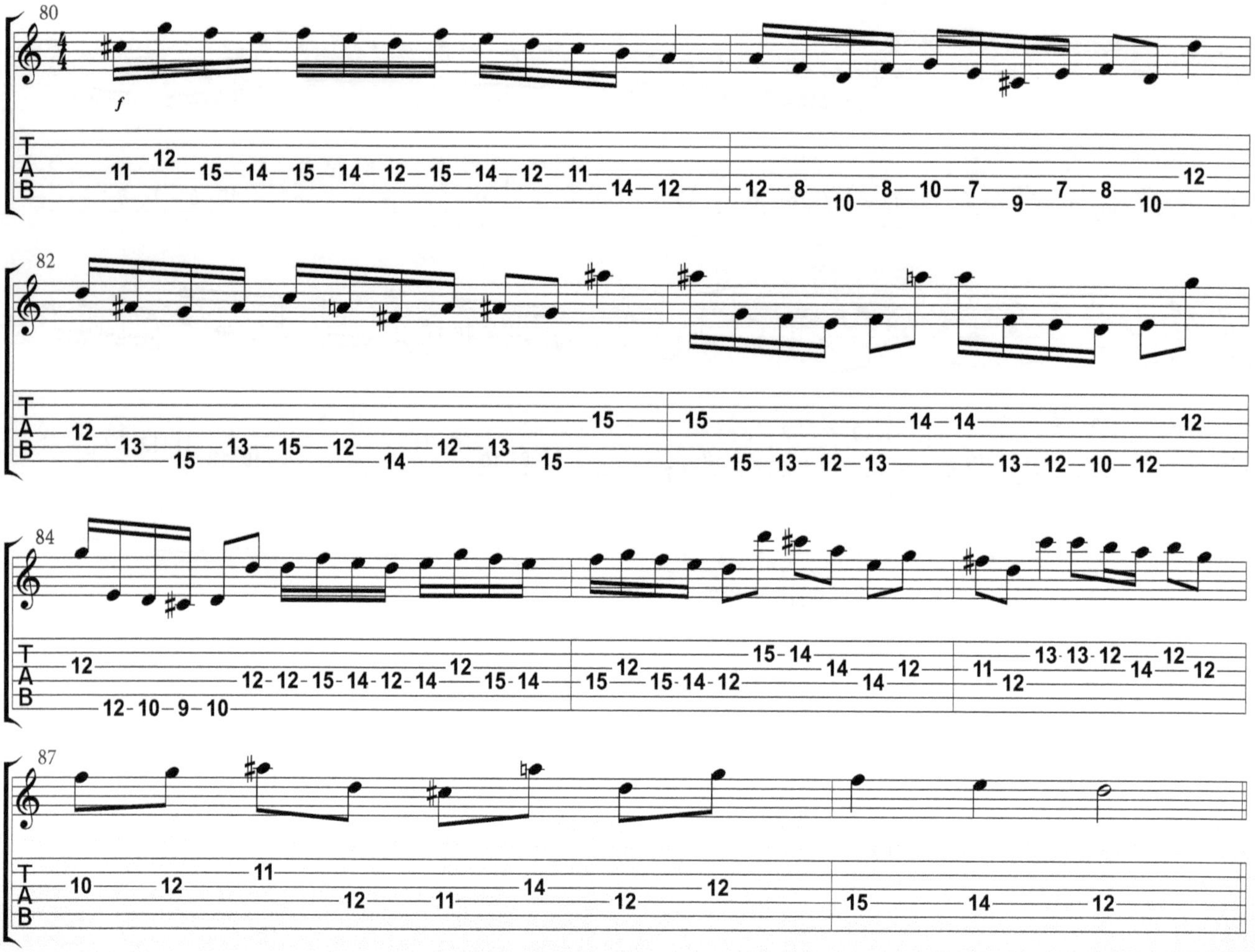

80

f

T A B: 11 12 15 14 15 14 12 15 14 12 11 14 12 | 12 8 10 8 10 7 9 7 8 10 12

82

T A B: 12 13 15 13 15 12 14 12 13 15 15 | 15 15 13 12 13 14 14 13 12 10 12 12

84

T A B: 12 12 10 9 10 12 12 15 14 12 14 12 15 14 | 15 12 15 14 12 15 14 14 14 12 | 11 12 13 13 12 14 12 12

87

T A B: 10 12 11 12 11 14 12 12 | 15 14 12

J.S. Bach

VIOLIN #2 for standard Guitar

26
f
28
30
mf
f
mf
f
32
mf
34
36
mf
f
39
41
mf

63
mf
f
mf
66
69
f
mf
71
73
75
77
82

84
mf
f
mf
TAB
11 12 15-14-15-14-12-15-14-12-11 14-12
12 12-15-14 16-12
12 15-14-12-14-10-12-14 10
87
TAB
10 13 12 13 10 12 13 10 12 13 12 10 13 12 10 9
10 12 11 12

Statue of J.S. Bach in Leipzig

DOUBLE BASS for baritone Guitar

25
28
31
34
37
40
43
46
f
TAB

48
f
TAB
51
54
58
62
65
68
71

74

f

TAB

5 — 4 — 0 — 3 — 0 — 2 — 3 | 3 — 5 — 3 — 1 | 1 — 8 — 7

77

TAB

5 — 5 — 3 | 3 — 5 — 5 | 6 — 3 — 4 — 2

80

TAB

7 — 5 — 7 — 7 — 4 — 5 | 5 — 5 — 3 | 3 — 5 — 5

83

TAB

3 — 3 — 1 — 2 | 5 — 5 — 7 — 5 — 4 — 5 | 5 — 4 — 5 — 7 — 8 — 7 — 8 — 5 — 7 — 5 — 7 — 8 — 7 — 5 — 8 — 7

86

TAB

5 — 4 — 5 — 7 — 5 — 3 — 6 — 5 — 3 — 2 — 3 — 5 — 3 — 1 — 0 — 3 | 2 — 1 — 1 — 3 — 2 — 3 — 4 | 3 — 1 — 3 — 5 — 5/3

"It's easy to play any musical instrument: all you have to do is touch the right key at the right time and the instrument will play itself"

-J.S.Bach

portrait of J.S. Bach

CELLO for standard Guitar

24
f
T
A
B
27
30
35
40
43
47
51

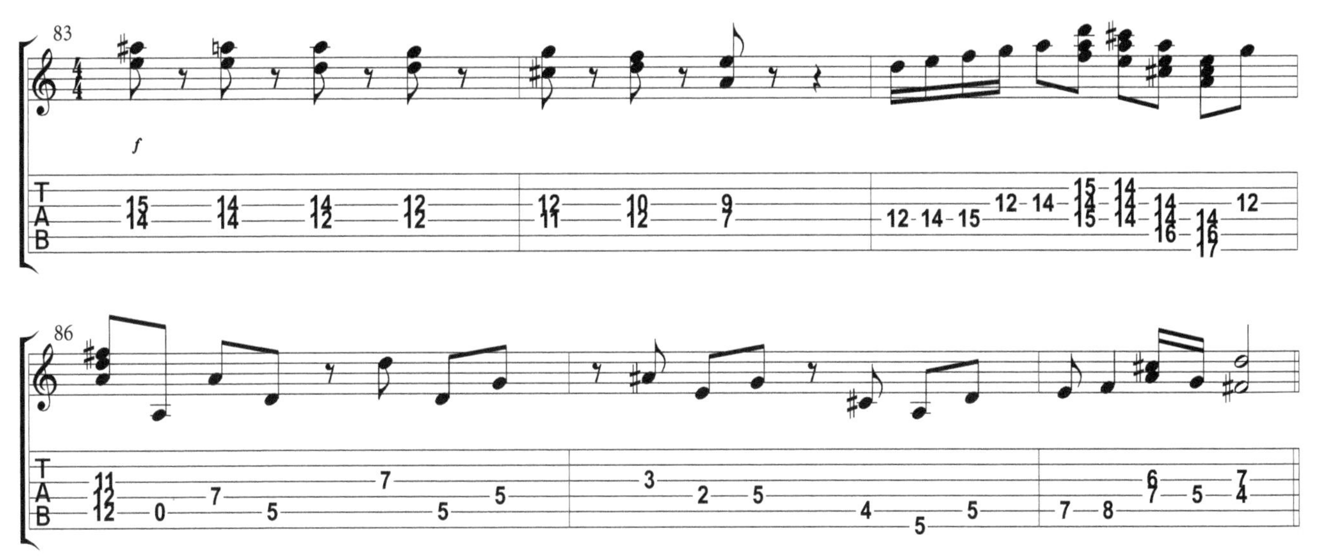
83
86
TAB

SCORE for Four Instruments

5
f
mf
f
mf
f
f
7
tr
tr

9
11
f
mf
T
A
B

13
f
mf
f
f
f
15

17
19

21
tr
f
tr
T
A
B
mf
f
f
23

25
27

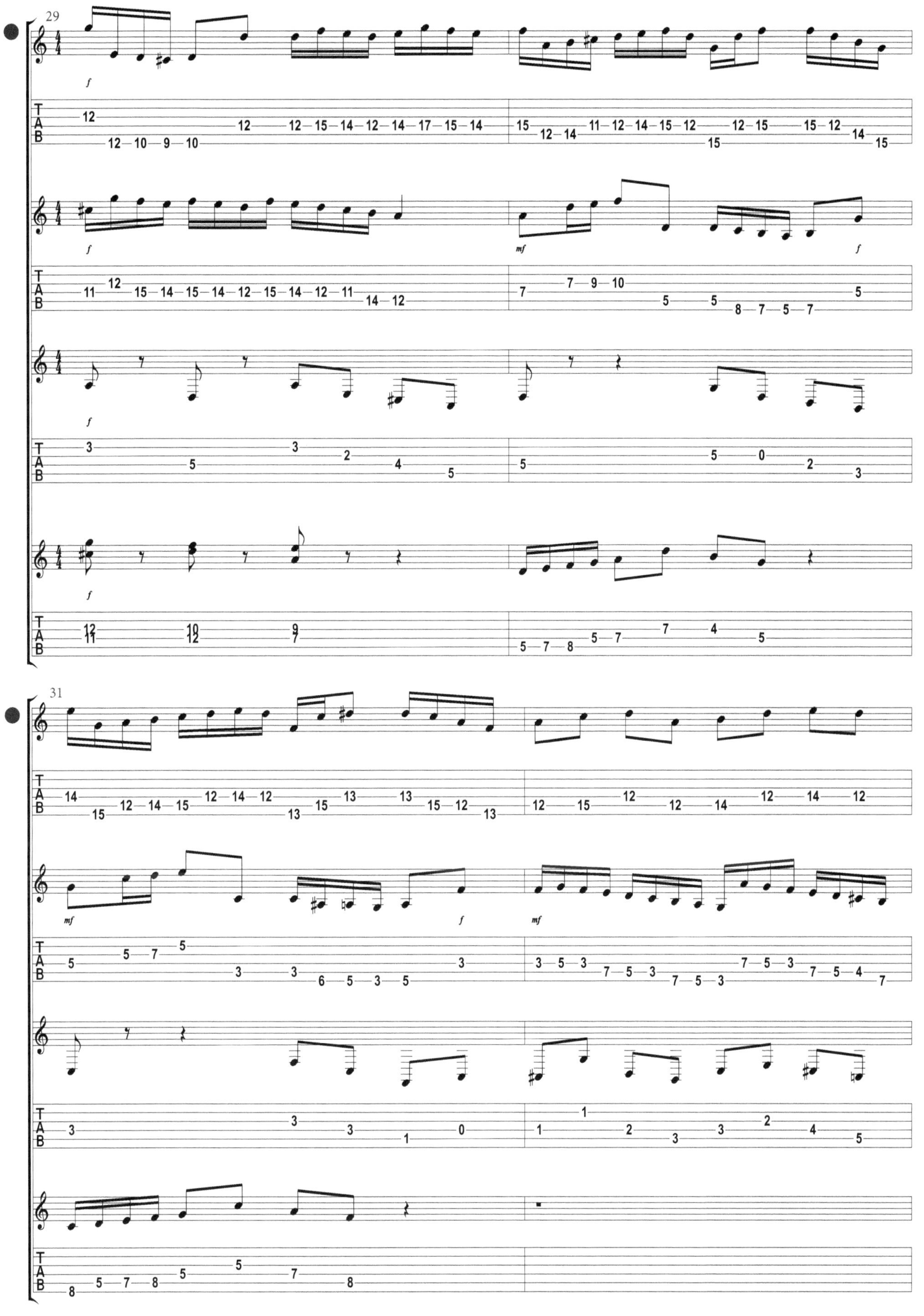
29
31

33
35

37
f
mf
f
f
f
39

41
f
mf
43
f
mf

49
tr
f
tr
f
mf
f
f
51
mp

53
f
mp
f
f
f
55
mp
f

57
T
A
B
59
mp
mf
f

61
f
mf
f
f
63
f

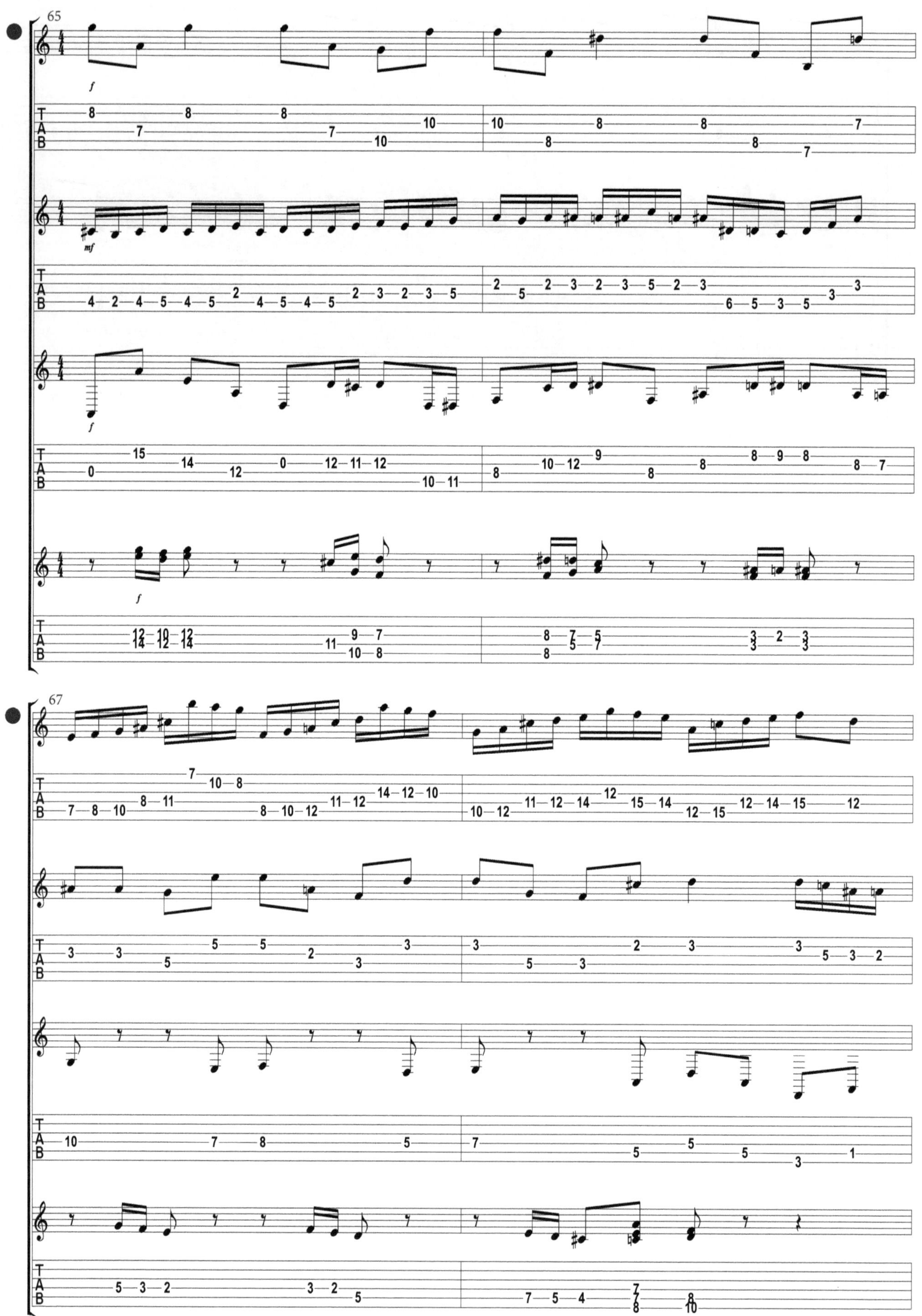
65
67

69
71

73
75

77
f
T
A
B
f
f
79
mf

81
f
mf
f
f
83

85
87

JOHANN
SEBASTIAN
BACH

FRETBOARD FLOW

Congratulations if you've made it through the entire score in all of it's parts. It's not exactly '*easy*' music to play but it's a great study, as are all of Bach's works. Of course this transcription is only one way that you can play it on a guitar. I'm not entirely happy with all the fingerings & postions that I had chosen for this piece. Not that they are bad, because they are all quite useable, but I want to encourage you to try to customize them in a way that suits your playing style. Not just in this Bach Concerto, but for all of the music that you play.

The thing is that when you arrange music like this, you want to do so in a way that 1st compliments the music and makes the music come to life. But you need to consider other things such as fingerings & position shifting as I had mentioned. I like to use the word "*flow*" a lot when talking about the hands motion as you are playing. Kind of like the saying "go with the *flow*". It's important that you pay attention to how you are moving around the guitar neck & that you are not fighting yourself to play your phrases. You always want to be thinking a few steps ahead & the direction you need to go to land in each preceding phrase.

Do your best to minimize your hand movement. Try to play as much as you can from within one single position. Generally, the less you have to move the easier it is for you to lock-in a solid pattern. When you have to shift positions too often, it's easy to lose stability & accuracy. So you always need to be thnking of ways that you can re-position your hand so that you can play more smoothly from note to note & phrase to phrase.

Sometimes you run into issues where you know that you need to make a large position shift; and obviously the farther you have to move your hand, the longer it will take to make the move. Try to figure out a way that you can work your way into a closer postion to avoid unnecessarily large position shifts. It's all about that '*flow*', being aware of where you are coming from & where you are going.

If you put some thought into the way your hand moves across the fretboard, you'll be able to eliminate a lot of the guess work in your playing. When you land solidly on a note, it should be because you've made an assessment of the notes that are played immediately before and after that note. You should know where you want to end up a split second before it's time to be there. As you practice a specific phrase, or even an entire Concerto like this one, you will be developing a flow that allows you to play the music fluently. If you find yourself struggling with a specific part, then work on just that part until you can play it cleanly. Then go back a few phrases and see if you can make the transition into & out of the trouble spot. A lot of times you'll find that you can play each individual part, but have a hard time making the connection/transition from part to part. If this is happening, re-think the way you are fretting the notes & ask yourself: "Is there a better way to play this?"

It's all common sense really. Just be aware that you may be able to re-group a phrase in a way that allows you to play it easier and more efficiently. The more you can do this the more proficient of a player you will be!

In the beginning of this Book, I had outlined three main themes from the Concerto. In the following pages I am going to give you some examples of how you can alter some of those themes (as well as some other selections) without changing the sound of the phrase. When I say change the sound of the phrase, I'm thinking more along the lines of the notes rather than the actual sound.

To be clear, as you move from string to string & position to position, although you may be hitting the same exact notes from the same octave, the timbre or color of the specific note will vary. For example, if you play your small E string open, it's the same note as if you play the E note on 19th fret of the A string. But the open small E string will have a much 'brighter' sound than the 19th fret/ A string E note will have. For one thing, the smaller the string is, the 'brighter' it will sound. And when you move up & down the neck position-wise, you'll hear a wide range of various colors and tones. So keep this in mind as well if you find that a phrase isn't sounding like you would like it to. Try to use a different position, set of strings, etc,,, to play the same part. You'd probably be surprised how much better certain phrases sound when played in better suited positions. Give it a try, and you will see & hear for yourself what I mean.

J.S. Bach Guitar Music

variation #1

T A B: 5 7 8 5 7 7 6 7 7 5 | 4 5 5

variation #2

T A B: 5 2 3 5 2 3 2 2 2 5 | 4 5 5

variation #3

T A B: 5 7 3 5 7 7 6 7 7 0 | 4 0 5

variation #4

T A B: 0 2 3 0 2 3 2 2 2 0 | 4 0 5

variation #5

T A B: 10 7 8 10 7 7 11 7 7 10 | 9 10 10

variation #6

T A B: 10 12 8 10 12 12 11 12 12 10 | 9 10 10

variation #7

T A B: 10 12 13 10 12 12 11 7 7 10 | 9 5 5

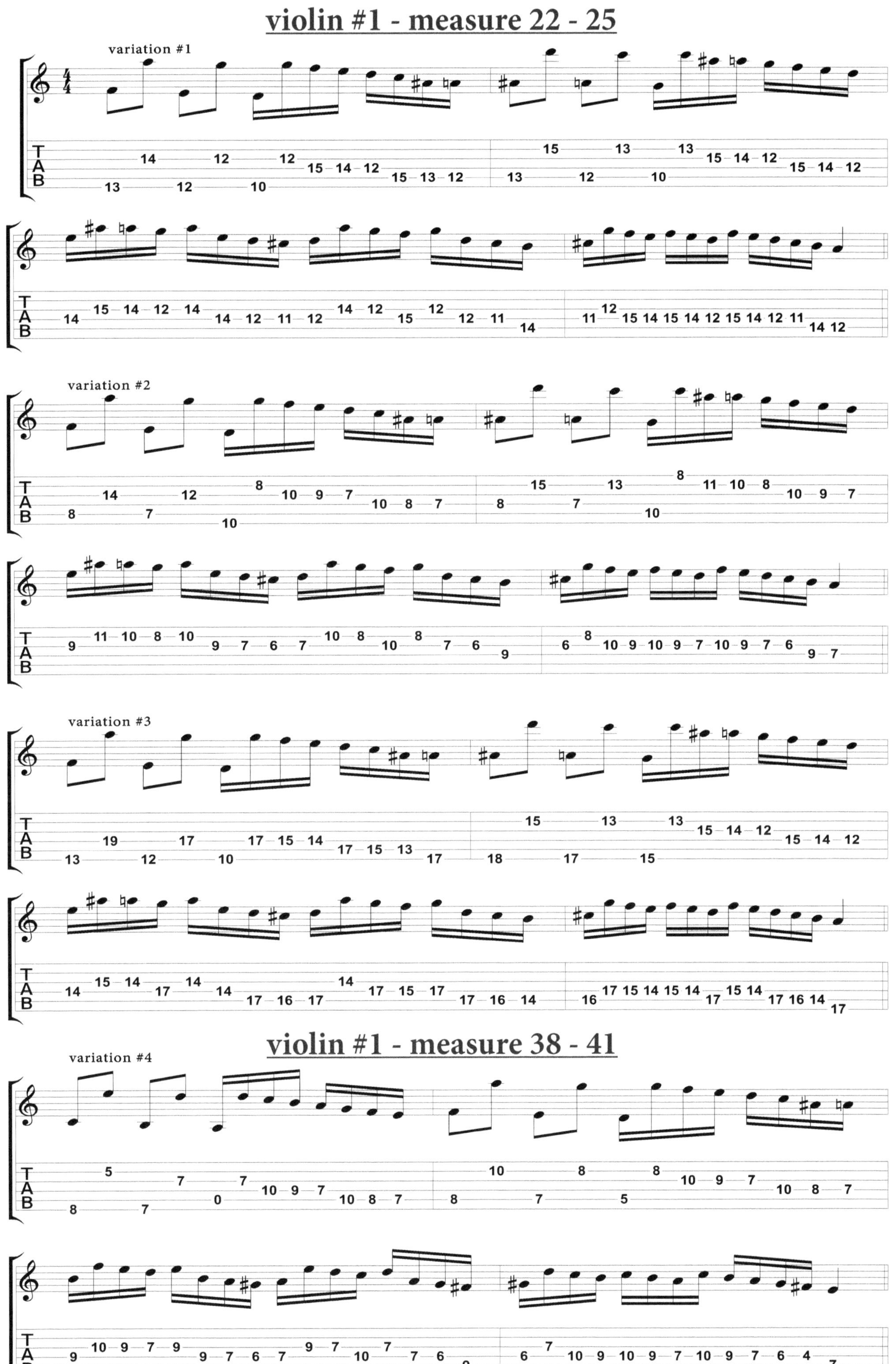
violin #1 - measure 22 - 25
variation #1
variation #2
variation #3
violin #1 - measure 38 - 41
variation #4

violin #2 - measure 65 - 66

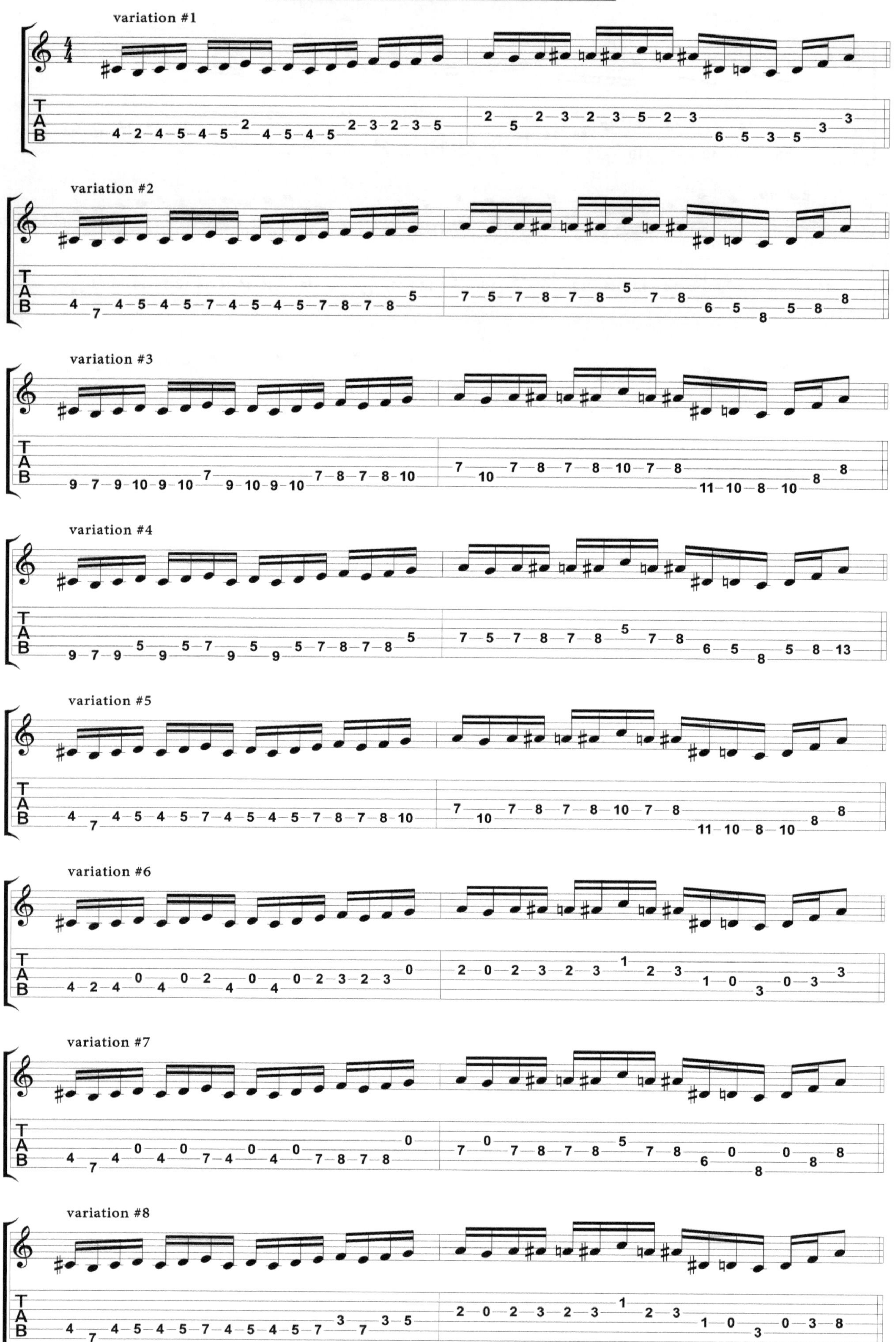

violin #2 - measure 44 - 45

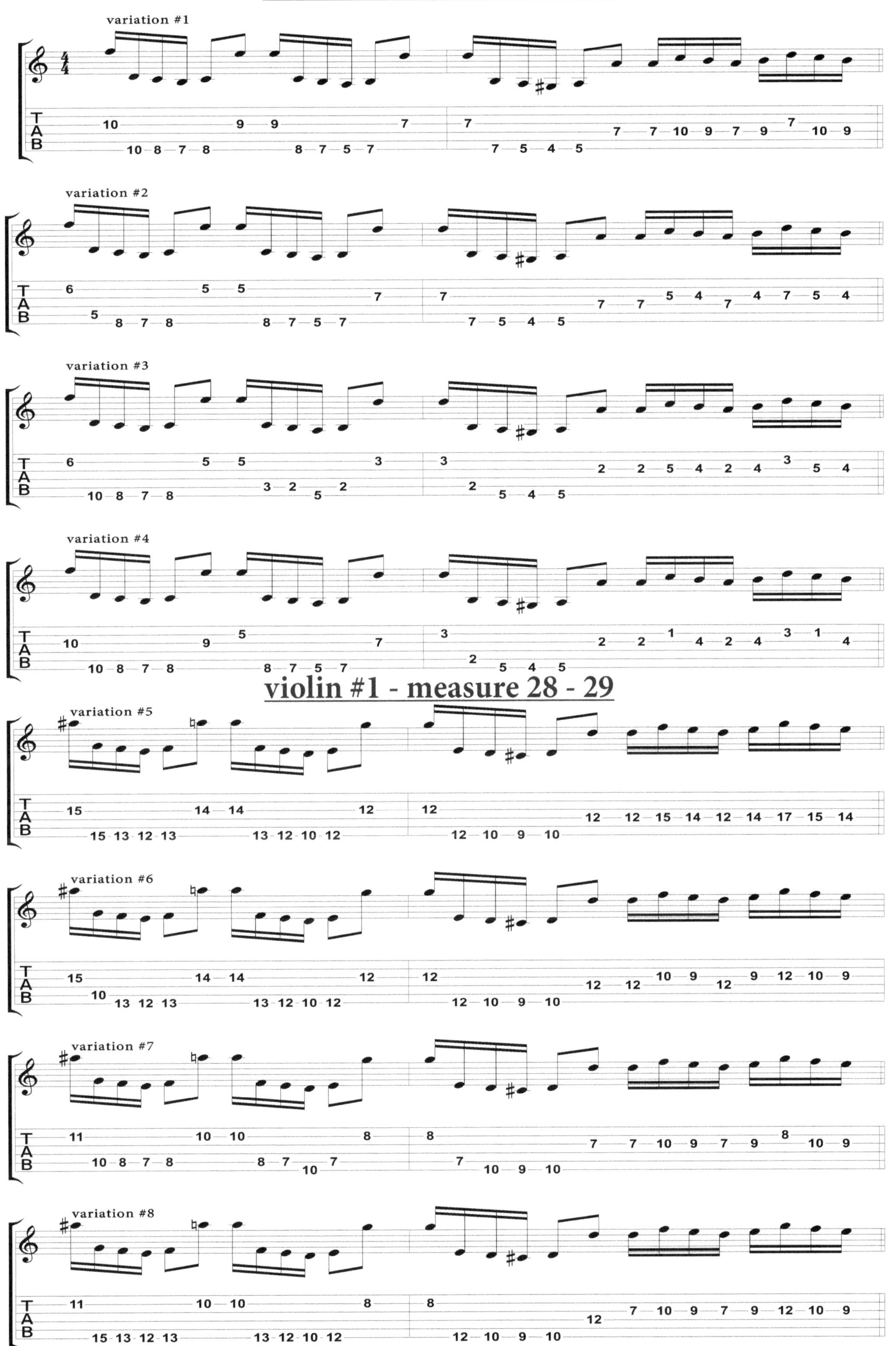

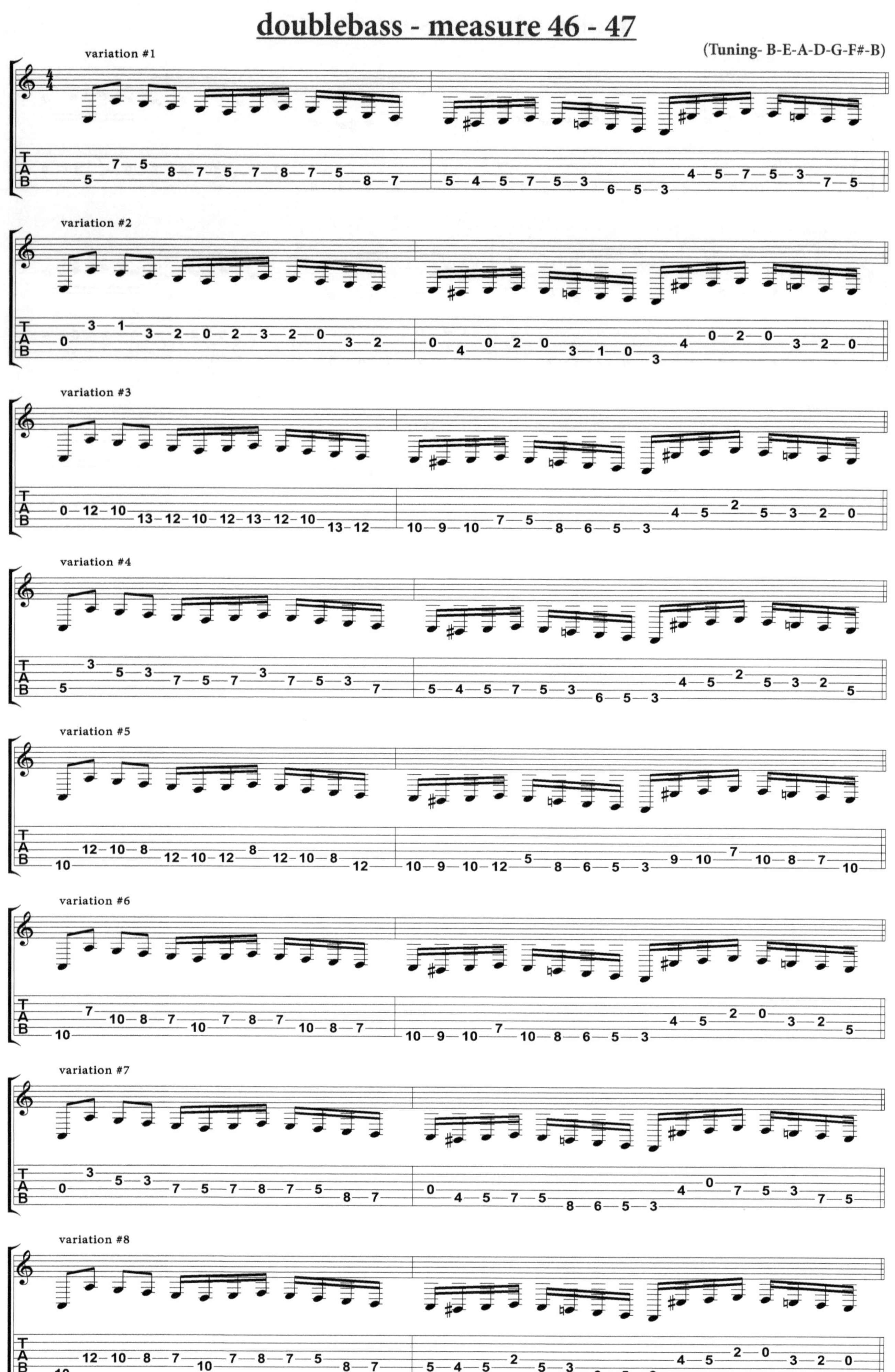
doublebass - measure 46 - 47
(Tuning- B-E-A-D-G-F#-B)
variation #1
variation #2
variation #3
variation #4
variation #5
variation #6
variation #7
variation #8

cello - measure 28 - 29

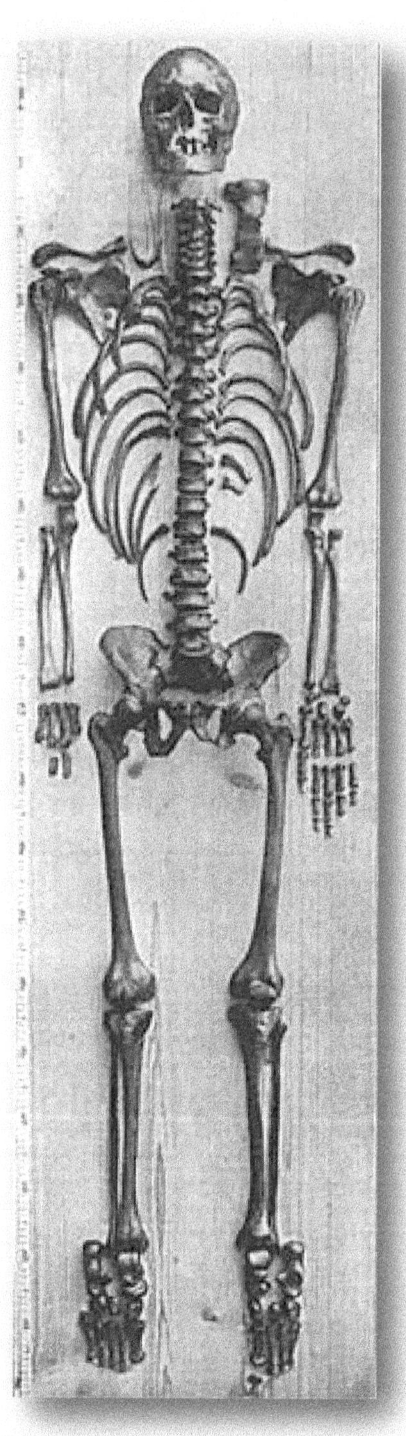

the skeleton of J.S. Bach

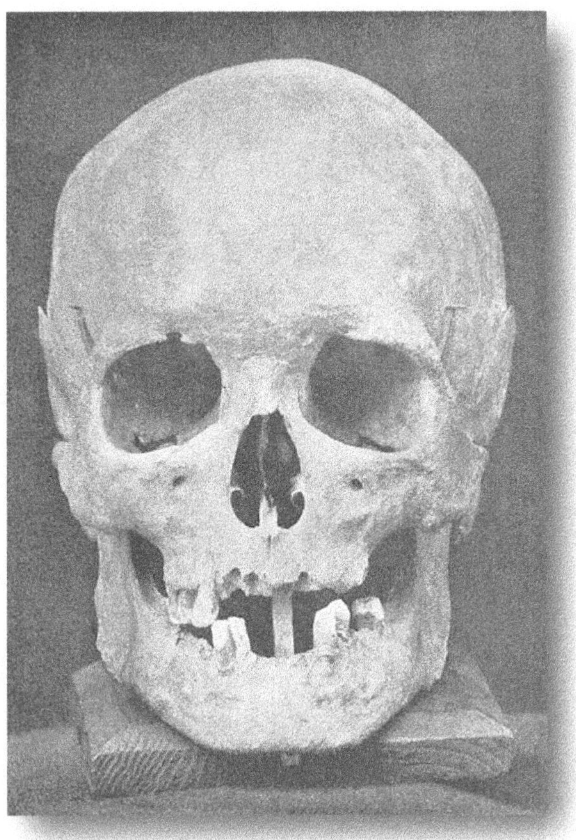

the skull of J.S. Bach

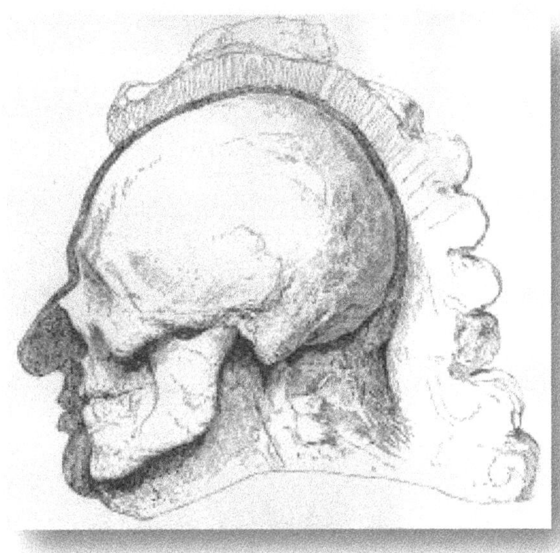

Seffner's sketch of the skull of J.S. Bach from which he later made a statue with.

Bach's handwriting for the 3rd Brandenburg Concerto in G Score

THE LEGACY OF J.S. BACH

What remains of Johann Sebastian Bach today is much more than just a few fragments of bones and a familiar name. He has left behind a legacy of immeasurable wealth for us all to study, learn from, be inspired by, and to enjoy. The complete known works of Bach have stood the test of time; over 300 years and his impression on humanity is still solidly rooted into the fabric of our present day.

His life's work serves as a model to demonstrate what we can accomplish within our own lifetime if only we are inclined to make an honest effort. The man's work ethic was incredible! And the merit of his work is apparent when considering the high place his name & his music holds, and maintains to this very day. He has earned his place through a lifetime of hardwork, and unquestionable genius. I can only stand by, humbly admiring what he has accomplished. For all the time I've personally spent on this Double Concerto alone, he's imagined, created, & documented at least a thousand more just as great. Of course he is only one of many great composers & men who have passed through in our history, but what an impact he has made!

LONG LIVE THE GREAT WORKS OF JOHANN SEBASTIAN BACH!!!

BWV 1043
1st Movement/Vivace
J.S.BACH
DOUBLE VIOLIN CONCERTO
in D minor for 4 Guitars
by- Jim Ross
Also available
• 1 FINGER EXERCISES FOR THE FRETTING HAND
• 2 FINGER EXERCISES FOR THE FRETTING HAND
• 3 FINGER EXERCISES FOR THE FRETTING HAND
• 4 FINGER EXERCISES FOR THE FRETTING HAND
• THE 1-2-3-4 FINGER GUITAR SYSTEM COMPLETE
with many more titles available soon
jimrossprojects

www.ingramcontent.com/pod-product-compliance
Ingram Content Group UK Ltd.
Pitfield, Milton Keynes, MK11 3LW, UK
UKHW050614260726
13967UKWH00008B/2858